MUMTASTIC

WHY YOU'RE SO AWESOME

This edition published in 2022
By SJG Publishing, HP22 6NF, UK

Author: Helen Vaux
Cover design: Milestone Creative
Contents design: Seagulls

978-1-913004-37-8

Printed in China

10 9 8 7 6 5 4 3 2 1

Contents

Introduction 4

10 reasons why mums rule the roost 6

Mums always hold it together 9

From your grown-up children... 12

When dad says 'no', mum says... 14

Top 10 mum superpowers 16

Things to do whilst waiting in the car 19

Bluff it: baking 21

Mum jokes 24

It's a fact! 25

Dos and don'ts of mum fashion 27

Mums on the big screen 30

All about you 33

Bluff it: multi-tasking 34

10 reasons your kids are amazing! 37

Mumisms 40

What kids really think... 42

All about you 44

Treat yourself: sleep 45

Mum jokes 48

Things mums would never say 49

Mum, please don't ever... 51

Mums on the page 52

It's a fact! 55

Songs about mum 57

It's a myth! 59

Our hero: real-life supermums 62

All about you 64

Bluff it: crafting 65

Treat yourself: face yoga 68

Don't ask your kids 72

For the mum who has everything 74

Mum jokes 76

10 ways to give yourself a break 77

All about you 81

It's a fact! 82

Bluff it: popular culture 84

Chat up lines for single mums 87

What type of mum are you? 89

A mum's guide to texting 94

The last word 96

Introduction

"A mother's love for her child is like nothing else in the world. It knows no law, no pity, it dares all things and crushes down remorselessly all that stands in its path."

Agatha Christie

What is it that makes mums 'mumtastic'?
Where on earth do we start?! A wonderful mum is
made up of a million different things. Think of mums
like stars twinkling in a night sky – we look up to them,
we wonder at their magic and they leave us in awe!
This book is here to tell mums everything about
what makes them the centre of our universe.

Every mum is different, but they all have something
in common – their children. And what do children all
have in common? They sometimes forget to let their
mums know how much they love them. Whether it's their
ability to pull a ten-course picnic out of their handbag or
their wizardry at time management (juggling three kids,
a full-time job and a penchant for boxsets), mums
deserve to be honoured to the hilt.

For all the mums that are feeling a bit tired and
underappreciated and are living for their next coffee, this
book is for you. By the end of the book, mums will feel
loved from the tops of their heads to the tips of their
toes. Mums, it's your turn to step into the spotlight
and shout: "I'm a mum and I'm utterly mumtastic!"

10 reasons why Mums
RULE THE ROOST

For a happy home, it's vital to know who's in charge – MUM. Their queenly skills? A sixth sense, eyes in the back of their heads and – just like MacGyver – coming up with clever solutions using just a cocktail stick and a strand of their hair.

1. Even when they're worrying about their big presentation at work and need to leave the house by 7am, their super sense knows exactly where to find that missing school gym sock.

2. They can produce a packed lunch from the dregs left in the refrigerator and make it look like it's been put together by a Michelin-starred chef.

3. Mums always tell you when you've dropped breakfast down your front – and can expertly assess the socially acceptable fine line between 'a quick wipe will do' and 'go and change'.

4. They've got great interior-design skills, despite the fact they never get time to sit down and read style magazines, and the last time 'DIY Dad' let them pick up a paintbrush was to help build a volcano for a school project.

5. They're the mother of all multitaskers. Mums can change a nappy with one hand, clean the bathroom with the other and take a call with their CEO – all whilst booking the next family holiday.

6. Mums make the best house rules – no shoes on the carpet, pick up your wet towels, no swearing – sadly we don't realize how necessary those rules are until we have a home of our own!

7. They know what you want before you've even asked for it. Whether it's a sixth sense, years of experience or having produced predictable children, they're always one step ahead.

8. Unlike anyone else in the house, they know that it's nicer to get into a made bed than one that looks like 20 elephants have played hockey in it.

9. Mums have an amazing ability to make five different dinners at the same time, just to keep everyone in the house happy.

10. Mums never give up – especially when it comes to reminding us to put the toilet seat down and eat with our mouths closed.

Mums always
HOLD IT TOGETHER

Sometimes there's gritted teeth,
sometimes a fake smile, yet mums have
a knack of holding it together even when
their patience is pushed to the limits.
Mums know that falling to pieces won't
get things done – and can 100% nail
a straight face when...

... the children smear the new carpet (and themselves) with the entire contents of a tube of Dad's haemorrhoid cream.

... Grandma starts a sentence with "I don't want to interfere but...".

... they find the letter about the school bake sale on the day of the said sale and have to decant a packet of cheap biscuits into a Tupperware container.

... they pick chocolate up off the floor... and then realize it's not chocolate.

... their dearest youngest child throws the mother of all tantrums at the supermarket in front of the person who'll make the decision on their promotion.

... they discover that their well-hidden secret stash of chocolate has 'disappeared'.

... Dad goes on a business trip and calls from the airport because he's forgotten his passport and needs Mum to deliver it to him.

... their toddler nephew grinds wet, chewed Haribo into the sofa cushions and then tries to lick them back off.

... an enormous bird with a gyppy tummy uses their line of clean, white washing as target practice.

... they open their lunch box at work to find their child's jam sandwiches and cheese strings – and not the avocado and salmon salad they'd been thinking about all morning.

... their passive-aggressive neighbour asks for the umpteenth time if everything's okay as she's "heard a lot of noise from the children".

... they discover that one of the children has drawn a rude image in the dirt on the back of the car, and they've been driving around with it there all day.

... their favourite (and most expensive) bubble bath has been emptied down the plughole because the packaging was required for a school project.

... they have to buy their own Mother's Day gift!

From your
GROWN-UP CHILDREN

Dear Mum
Thank you for not...

....

... insisting that we only wore the clothes you made, even though we knew how much you loved your sewing machine.

... tolerating my fussy eating, meaning I can now go to restaurants and eat like a grown-up.

... trying to choose my friends for me, and
for letting me make mistakes so that I'm
a better judge of character now.

... stopping hugging me when I was a rude,
disrespectful and downright foul teenager.
(I loved your hugs then and still do now.)

... saying "I told you so" every time I made a
truly awful relationship decision and ended
up crying in my room for days.

... giving up on me when I confused not listening
to you with being independent.

... taking it to heart all those times I said
something mean to you and called you
"the worst mum in the world".

... thinking you always had to give me a solution
– your being with me and saying "I love you"
was enough, and still is.

When dad says "No"
MUM SAYS...

... YES, or at least MAYBE! If dads say "no" then there must be a good reason – thankfully though, mums have a clever knack of thinking around a problem for everyone's benefit.

....

Car... Dad moans about the expense of insurance and refuses to let you drive his pride and joy. Mum has her eye on someone to taxi her to and from her girls' nights out. She's done an awful lot of taxiing – it's payback time.

Money... Dad thinks you're going to waste it on rubbish you don't need. Mum knows that being in charge of your finances and understanding the value of money (when you discover how wasteful it is to spend it badly) will stand you in good stead in the future.

New clothes... Dad suggests you can get at least 10 years' more wear from your current clothes – after all, that's always worked for him. Mum spies an excuse to take you out shopping and accidentally use her credit card on a few purchases for herself.

Mobile phone upgrade... Dad wants to know what's wrong with having a brick of a phone like his. Mum knows that the latest model has enhanced tracking capability and a feature that wraps you in cotton wool if you're in danger. (Well, she'd like it to...)

Holiday with friends... Dad remembers his holiday with the lads when he was 18 – and exactly what he got up to. Mum has the same thought as Dad – but then weighs it all up against having peace and quiet at home for a week.

Staying out past midnight... Dad is not staying up until 1am to come and collect you – nor is he prepared to pay for a taxi. Mum remembers that she often didn't come home at all – but you do still need to send her a text and evidence that you are where you say you are.

Top 10 Mum
SUPERPOWERS

When a woman becomes a mum, something magical happens. No one knows how or why they are the chosen ones, just that they take on incredible, superhuman abilities.

1. Mums can spot a potential spillage at 500 metres and can take the necessary swift action to prevent the spillage occurring.

2. A mum can hear about someone's school day, take a work call and change lanes – all at the same time as making a 'friendly' gesture to the driver that's just cut her up.

3. They are able to detect the slightest peep from a child who's woken up in the middle of the night, even over the noise of her partner's snoring.

4. They always know the right thing to say. And what *not* to say. AND their timing is impeccable. This can mean only one thing – mums are mind readers.

5. Why just have eyes in the front and back of your head when you can have them ALL AROUND your head. Nothing gets past a mum. Not even a flea in an invisibility cloak.

6. Whenever something is needed, it's in Mum's bag. Like Mary Poppins, mums' bags contain an endless supply of useful items – tissues, a spare sweater, snacks, plasters. Need a wheel jack and a spare tyre? Ask Mum. It'll be in her bag.

7. Mums provide a warm, nourishing home for a tiny human being for nine months, then push it out through an incredibly sensitive (and tiny) part of their body. *Ta da!*

8. Oh, and they provide a warm, nourishing home for a growing human being for at least 18 years (generally longer), then push it out through the front door. *Ta ra!*

9. Magic kisses. Who needs medicine when Mum can simply 'kiss it better'? Scientists have been working for years to try to bottle whatever the special chemical is in mothers' saliva. Some have even called it the holy grail of the medical world.

10. Mums have an unbelievably high tolerance of anything that comes out of their children's mouths. From chewed-up broccoli to car sick to insults hurled as a teenager slams a door, mums simply ride the wave and produce a tissue from their magical bag.

Things to do whilst WAITING IN THE CAR

Mums spend a vast amount of time waiting in cars. School pick-ups, clubs, birthday parties – you name it, mums have sat outside it. Put down your phone and try these tips for using the time wisely.

....

Write a book. If you've got something interesting to say, let the world know. You've got some great material with those ballet mums if you let your imagination run wild!

19

Take a free online course. What have you always wanted to learn but never got round to? It doesn't have to be something useful – make it something you love.

Read a book. SO obvious but something mums often struggle to make time for. Unless you commute to work by bus or train, spare time to read gets eaten up by all those other things you think you *should* be doing. Escape with a great book and time will fly.

Catch up on school correspondence. Raffle prizes needed! There's someone with head lice in the middle school again! Set aside this time to deal with it all in one go and put dates to remember in your calendar.

Face yoga. Want to try 10 unbelievably easy exercises to get rid of a double chin? Yes, please! Just make sure no one can see you. Turn to page 68 to find out more...

Do a digital detox. Tired of seeing photos of an ex-colleague's cat on Facebook? Delete them. Another email with 10% off the maternity bras you bought 10 years ago? Unsubscribe. You'll be surprised what a difference ditching digital clutter makes to your head space.

Meditate. Did you know that just 10 minutes of meditation a day can bring positive benefits? Reduce stress and anxiety, improve focus and grow into your best self.

Bluff it:
BAKING

Things have moved on since the 1950s housewife had dinner on the table when her husband got home. Yet there are some outdated perceptions that persist: namely, that all mums can bake. If you need to produce something wondrous for a cake sale, here's how to bluff your way through.

Does a recipe tell you to bake something blind? Whatever you do, don't put on a blindfold and attempt to bake by touch. To 'bake blind' means baking the crust of a pie/tart without the filling.

Pastry is notoriously hard to get right, so why try when someone can do it for you? Any decent-sized supermarket has a range of ready-made pastry in their refrigerated section. There's no need to feel embarrassed about cheating. No one will ever know. Unless you tell them – so don't.

Minimize the risk of setting off your smoke alarm by choosing a no-bake recipe. Cheesecakes are always a good option and generally require no more skill than crushing some biscuits into little pieces. The biggest risk with a no-bake recipe is not leaving enough time for it to chill. But at least it won't be burned.

Sadly, baking a cake isn't like making a stew. With a stew, you can dump whatever you like in the pot and if it's too watery at the end, you just add some cornflour. Baking is annoyingly precise, so make sure you measure everything out EXACTLY. An extra ounce of this or that will completely throw the recipe out. Digital scales are your friend.

Dropped eggshell in the cake mix?? Don't panic!
Wet your finger and place it near the shell. It will magically
gravitate towards your finger, making it easier to remove it.
Plus, eggshells sink when baked, which means you might be
able to find them later. (This doesn't work with a fingernail
though, so if that's your issue, start over again.)

Owning a rolling pin isn't a prerequisite of being a mother.
Thankfully, having a couple of bottles of wine lying around is.
If you need to roll out some pastry and don't have the traditional
equipment to hand, a wine bottle will do a perfectly adequate job.

That's the way the cookie crumbles – well, it does if you're
not patient. When you take cookies out of the oven, leave them
to rest on the baking sheet for one minute before you move
them to a wire cooling rack. By doing that, the heat has
a chance to escape, and the cookies are less likely to
become a pile of crumbs when you lift them.

Uneven and misshapen cupcakes? Use an ice-cream scoop for
putting the cupcake batter in the paper cases. One scoop is
exactly the right size for a single cupcake. Job done.

Mum JOKES

Why did the cookie cry?
Because his mother was a wafer so long!

Daughter: Mum, what's it like to have the
greatest daughter in the world?
Mother: I don't know, Sweetheart. Ask your grandmother.

How many mums does it take to screw in a light bulb?
One, obviously. And she has to do it or else it won't get done.

The mother who gives birth to the largest baby on Earth is a mother elephant. After a long 22-month pregnancy, she gives birth to a 200-pound calf. Eye-watering.

One of the oldest mothers in modern history to give birth is Rajo Devi Lohan from India. Rajo was 70 years old when she gave birth to a baby girl in 2008 following IVF treatment.

Actor Leonardo DiCaprio was apparently named Leonardo because his pregnant mother was looking at a Leonardo da Vinci painting in a museum in Italy when she felt her son's first kick.

In the US, Mother's Day started in 1908 and was the creation of Anna Jarvis. Anna wanted to remember her mother, who had sadly passed away, and requested that her friends wore white carnations to church.

In the UK, Mothering Sunday has been around since the 16th century. Originally, it was more of a religious festival, celebrated on the fourth Sunday in Lent, a day for thanking mums. Inspired by Anna Jarvis in the US, Constance Penswick-Smith brought back Mothering Sunday in 1914.

Women speak approximately 20,000 words per day. This compares to 7,000 per day for men. A University of Maryland study connects this to the higher levels of a protein found in the female brain. This protein is called 'FOXP2', also known as the 'language protein'.

Dos and don'ts of
MUM FASHION

The biggest fashion danger for mums? Dressing like ALL the other mums! It's very easy to follow the crowd, but it doesn't have to be like that...

Do

Wear 'mum jeans' – they were named for you, after all. Inspired by the 90s, these high-waisted heroes are back in fashion so don't feel pressured to squeeze into skinnies. Comfortable can be cool!

Check out brands before you buy. Brands that look super-cool to you might be the height of chav fashion and leave your kids rolling around on the floor laughing.

Find your own style. Wear what makes you happy – it really doesn't matter what other people think. They'll most likely look at you and wish they had the confidence to do the same!

Have key pieces that mix and match with each other. If you can get dressed in the dark and still look great, you've cracked it. Go for quality (and that means things you love, rather than expensive items) over quantity.

Use accessories like scarves, belts and statement necklaces. Adding one of these items can completely change the look of an outfit. In fact, you could wear the same outfit for a whole week with different accessories and no one would bat an eyelid!

Don't

Wear big logos. Keep your logos discreet and classy. Just like you!

Buy loads of cheap shoes to suit any occasion. If there's one thing to invest in, it's shoes. Having a small collection of good-quality shoes will last you far longer than 50 pairs of cheap, plastic ones.

Buy something just because it's in fashion and all the other mums have jumped on the bandwagon. Does the style suit them all? Probably not, and it might not suit you. Everyone has a different body shape that works with different styles – don't wear something that doesn't flatter you just to run with the pack!

Over-accessorize. Layered necklaces might be 'in' but don't combine them with ear chandeliers unless you want people to hear you before they see you.

Follow your teenager daughter's style tips. Young girls' fashions are not made for a grown woman's body!

Buy or keep anything just in case it fits you one day. Life's too short. Enjoy the body you're in and dress to make the most of it.

Mums on the
BIG SCREEN

Parenting – along with love and
bank heists – is a perennial favourite
of the movie industry. Mums are so
wonderful, we just can't stop making
movies about them. From the hilarious
to the heartfelt, here are some great
films guaranteed to give you the feels.

Juno (2007) – Faced with an unplanned pregnancy, a young woman makes an unusual decision regarding the unborn child.

Bad Moms (2016) – When newly single mother, Amy, snaps under the weight of responsibility, two other burned-out mums join her on a spree of bad behaviour. Hilarious – especially if you're familiar with school mum 'politics'.

Boyhood (2014) – Filmed over 12 years, the story of a single mother raising her son and daughter against all odds.

Lion (2016) – The true story of a five-year-old boy who gets lost at a train station in India. Years after being adopted, he sets out to find his birth mother and the hometown he left behind.

The Joy Luck Club (1993) – Four women who left their homeland and made America their home have to adjust their parenting style and behaviour, thus changing their relationships with their daughters.

Mask (1985) – Based on a true story, Cher plays a bohemian biker mum determined to provide a normal life for her son, who has a rare medical condition.

Alice Doesn't Live Here Anymore (1974) – An aspiring singer is forced to take a job as a waitress in a run-down diner to support herself and her young son. Driven by a female role – rare for a Scorsese film!

All About My Mother (1999) – Pedro Almodovar's Oscar-winning comedy-drama about a single mother dealing with the death of her teenage son.

Lady Bird (2017) – A hard-working mother must deal with her strongly opinionated and rebellious teenage daughter. (Sound familiar?!)

Mamma Mia! (2008) – A girl preparing for her wedding invites her three possible fathers to the ceremony without telling her mum. Fab ABBA soundtrack – if you can excuse Pierce Brosnan's singing!

Because I Said So (2007) – A comedy about a complex but sweet relationship between a mum and her three daughters. Two daughters are married, while one is single and looking for love – so Mum steps in.

Mother's Day (2016) – Romantic comedy following the lives of strangers as they celebrate Mother's Day in their own way, revealing the ways in which their lives are intertwined.

All about YOU

"When you are a mother, you are never really alone
in your thoughts. A mother always has to think twice,
once for herself and once for her child."

SOPHIA LOREN

"There was never a child so lovely but his mother
was glad to get him to sleep."

RALPH WALDO EMERSON

"Motherhood is not for the faint-hearted. Frogs, skinned knees,
and the insults of teenage girls are not meant for the wimpy."

DANIELLE STEEL

Bluff it:
MULTITASKING

Multitasking – a mum superpower!
Or is it? Sometimes, multitasking
becomes simply trying to do too much
at once and ending up in a kerfuffle.
There's a fine line between juggling lots of
balls and making a balls-up. These tips will
help you get more done by doing less.

Make lists. Lots of lists. Then prioritize each list and make a list of all the priorities on the lists. The biggest benefit of a list is that you get everything that is swirling around inside your head down onto paper. This 'brain declutter' will reduce your stress levels. Who knows, you might even tick some items off your list.

Know your limits! Of course, with multitasking, having only two hands is NOT a limit. But there are only 24 hours in a day and presumably you'd like to spend some of those sleeping. Learn to say "no" when you're asked to do something that you know will be the drop of water that makes your bucket overflow. Nothing lets your inability to multitask out of the bag more than saying you'll do something for someone and then not doing it.

If you find yourself in a tizz and don't know where to start, you need to prioritize! Order your tasks so that 'important' sets the tone, rather than 'urgent'. So:

Important and urgent – e.g. taking your sick dog to the vet.

Important but not urgent –
e.g. booking next year's summer holiday.

Not important but urgent –
e.g. getting your nails done before the party.

Not important and not urgent – e.g. cleaning the car.

Become a champion of single-tasking. Doing one thing at a time is infinitely more productive than multitasking. Switching between tasks is pretty exhausting for the brain, so focus on the task in hand. You'll get it done more quickly – and better – because it has your full attention. No one needs to know you're not multitasking. To all appearances you are because you're getting more done, faster!

Block out distractions. Faffing is the enemy of getting stuff done. Put your phone on silent, bury it in a hole in the garden – whatever you need to do to focus and get some peace and quiet. There are also some great apps available that can limit your faff time on websites. Cold turkey may give you the shakes, but you'll be amazed how much you get done. Providing it doesn't require the internet...

10 reasons your kids are AMAZING!

In a book all about mums, let's not forget who made them who they are – their children! While you're desperately trying to set boundaries and make them obey your rules, remember: parenting is a two-way adventure...

1. They keep you healthy! Studies have shown that people with children have lower blood pressure than those without – mind you, you might feel differently as you sink into a chair at the end of the day, glass of wine in hand. (Just make it red wine: better for the heart.)

2. They curb your spending. New winter coat for you or new sports kit for the kids? Ponder that for a moment... Unless you want the guilt and the moaning, it's got to be the sports kit.

3. They teach you things you didn't know and would be scared to Google. ("Is that even a thing?" "Do people really do *that*?") If you thought there was nothing your kids could surprise you with, think again.

4. You can use them to get out of social events. There's nothing so useful as a 'babysitter letting you down' to avoid the evening out that seemed like such a good idea when you accepted the invitation.

5. They toughen you up. Forget military training, being a mum teaches you resilience and the ability to handle all the challenges that parenthood throws at you – even when you're ill or sleep deprived.

6. They remind you to stop and smell the roses. We lose our sense of wonder as we get older – but see a toddler get excited about a bubble machine or a ladybird on a flower and you soon realize how important it is to appreciate the small things.

7. They remind you what unconditional love is – how to accept it and how to give it. It's love like you've never felt before!

8. They show you how to be brave. Whether it's watching your child do something outside their comfort zone or having to do something you're not comfortable with to show your child that it's okay, courage is a natural by-product of being a parent.

9. They release your inner child. Why do adults think they're too old to play?! It's a fantastic way to focus your mind and ignore the humdrum of everyday life. Forget the grocery shopping and the laundry and build something with Lego bricks.

10. They'll look after you when you're old and decrepit. As you park your mobility scooter outside the bungalow you've downsized to, you'll realize all the time and money you spent on them was worth it!

Mumisms

Mums have a nugget of wisdom for every occasion – whether it's asked for or not. When something important is on the line, 'mum knows best', so reject her advice at your peril! Here are some of the phrases mums love to say (and repeat *ad infinitum*)...

....

"What part of 'no' don't you understand?"

"If they told you to jump off a cliff, would you?"

"It hurts me more than it hurts you."

"I don't care who started it!"

"If you're too full to finish your dinner, you're too full for dessert."

"When you have your own house, you can make the rules."

"Do you think your socks are going to pick themselves up?"

"What did you father say?"

"A little birdie told me!"

"DO NOT put that in your mouth. You don't know where it has been!"

"Are you going out dressed like *that*?"

"When you have children of your own, you'll understand."

"Do what I say, not what I do."

"There's enough dirt in those ears to grow potatoes!"

"How do you know you don't like it if you've not even tried it?"

"If you're bored, I can always find something for you to do."

"Don't go out with wet hair. You'll catch a cold."

"Because I said so, that's why."

"What did I say the FIRST time?"

What kids
REALLY THINK...

Mums can sometimes feel like unsung heroes. But what would your kids say to you if they were being completely honest? Read on...

....

"Mum, I ignored it at the time, but I do still remember that advice you gave me – and it was absolutely spot on."

"When I told you I hated you, I was just annoyed you were right."

"Every time I rolled my eyes or tutted,
I was bonkers not to listen to you!"

"Thank you for not saying 'I told you so'
when I don't take your advice and you're right."

"I'm grateful for all the sacrifices –
large and small – you make for me."

"What an amazing grandma you're going to be!"

"You've taught me everything I know about being
organized – I never realized how much prep and packing
it took to simply get a child out of the house!"

"All those good habits you taught me that seemed silly at the
time – please/thank you, holding doors open, keeping my mouth
closed when eating – mean I'm not now one of those incredibly
annoying people who don't have those habits!"

"I've bought (and made) you some pretty awful gifts, so thank
you for always reacting like I'd presented you with a gold bar."

"Every time you wrapped me in a hug, I felt like
the safest, most loved person in the world."

"If I can be half the person you are, I'll be very happy indeed."

All about YOU

"Successful mothers are not the ones that have never struggled. They are the ones that never give up, despite the struggles."

SHARON JAYNES

"There will be so many times you feel like you've failed, but in the eyes, heart and mind of your child, you are super mom."

STEPHANIE PRECOURT

"There is nothing as sincere as a mother's kiss."

SALEEM SHARMA

Treat yourself: SLEEP

Being a mum brings wonderful benefits and moments of joy, but it does lose you sleep. Whether it's being up all hours with a crying newborn, trying to coax a toddler back into their bed or twitching the curtains as you wait for your teenager to return from a party, sleep can be hard to come by. Here's why – and how to get more of it!

The benefits of a good night's sleep

Sleep improves your memory and concentration.

It keeps your heart healthy.

It supports your immune system to stay strong.

Sleep helps reduce stress, lifts your mood and improves your mental health and emotional well-being.

It boosts learning. As we sleep, our brain processes the memories and information we've acquired during the day, filing them away so they're ready to recall in the future.

It makes you better able to handle the next day (with less shouting!).

How to get better sleep

Don't get stuck on the couch. Be firm about your bedtime routine. Set a go-to-bed alarm if necessary!

Declutter your bedroom. Get rid of all the bits and bobs that just gather dust and disrupt the zen! A bedroom should only be for sleep and sex.

Is your sleeping environment comfortable? If it's too hot, too light or too noisy, think about how you can fix it.

Give your bedroom a sense of calm by painting the walls in soothing, sleep-friendly colours – lavender, light grey, soft green, pale blue and light blue all have this effect.

Is it time to invest in a new mattress? As a general rule, mattresses should be replaced roughly every 10 years for the best sleep.

Follow the advice you give your kids and avoid using electronic devices before bedtime. The light from the screen can activate parts of your brain and keep you awake. Read or listen to music.

Try not to nap during the day. A power nap can be good for you but keep it short (20 mins) and don't do it after 3pm.

Avoid caffeine immediately before bedtime. The same goes for alcohol (sorry!). Whilst alcohol may make you feel sleepy, it lessens the quality of your sleep.

If worries are keeping you awake, try keeping a notebook by your bed. Jot down what you are worrying about – this will get it out of your head and postpone it until the next day when you're better able to deal with it.

Mum JOKES

Why did the mother cross the road?

To get some peace and quiet!

I bought my mum a card that said, "Happy Mother's Day from the World's Worst Son". I forgot to send it, but I think she knows.

What kind of boat is barely staying afloat,
yet somehow manages to function?

The mother ship.

Things mum would NEVER SAY

Parents can be fairly predictable when it comes to what they say to their children. After all, parents are all singing off the same 'my house, my rules' hymn sheet. How surprised would you be to hear yourself or your mum utter any of the statements below?!

....

"Leave all the lights on. It makes the house look more jolly."

"Take your time. It doesn't matter if we're late."

"Yes, that shirt will do another week without a wash.
You don't smell too bad."

"I haven't got a tissue. Use your sleeve."

"You look so adorable when you roll your eyes at me."

"I want you home by 10pm, but don't worry
if you're an hour or two late."

"Why don't you put on more make-up? I can still recognize you."

"Don't bother to hang up your wet towel. I love folding towels."

"Mother's Day? Oh, it's no big deal."

"Can you see the TV from all the way over there? Sit a bit closer."

"Your dad is such a brilliant dancer!"

"Of course one hour's notice isn't too late to
make a costume for World Book Day!"

"Keep your shoes on and kick back on the sofa."

"If you can't say something nice about a person, text it."

"Don't call to let me know you've got there safely."

"If you don't eat all your dinner, you'll have a space for dessert."

Mum, please
DON'T EVER...

... stop telling me I've got something on my face
(but do stop trying to wipe it off with a tissue and spit).

... read *Battle Hymn of the Tiger Mother*.

... stop texting me to remind me about family birthdays,
to check I'm dressing appropriately for the weather
and to prompt me to call you to chat properly.

... hesitate to invite me over for dinner, even when it seems
like I'm always busy with something else.

... show THAT baby photo to ANYONE I bring home to meet you.
The threat may be funny, but the reality is deeply embarrassing.

... listen to anyone who says you should do things differently
or better – you're already doing an amazing job.

... doubt that you're the most incredible,
awesome and wonderful mum ever.

51

Mums
ON THE PAGE

Motherhood – and what it means to be a mum – have long been popular subjects in literature. This is testimony to the importance of mums in our lives. They provide unconditional love, juggle home and work, and yet still find time to worry about whether they're doing a good job! So, mums, give yourself a break – put your feet up, hunker down and lose yourself in a book...

The Handmaid's Tale by Margaret Atwood – A dystopian novel, set in the near-future, where a dictatorship has stripped women of all their rights, and handmaids are assigned to bear children.

The Tenant of Wildfell Hall by Anne Brontë – The classic novel about the mystery of a beautiful, but reclusive, young widow who moves into the neighbourhood with her young son.

Wild Swans: Three Daughters of China by Jung Chang – The stories of three generations of women living through the tumult of 20th-century China.

Before We Visit the Goddess by Chitra Banerjee Divakaruni – A novel about three generations of mothers and daughters as the family moves from Bengal, India to America.

Room by Emma Donoghue – A kidnapped girl raises her son in captivity in a single room while planning their escape.

Chocolat by Joanne Harris – A young single mother and her daughter move to a French village and open a magical chocolaterie, transforming the lives of those around them.

Little Earthquakes by Jennifer Weiner – Three new mothers bond over their shared experience of struggling to raise babies.

Wild: From Lost to Found on the Pacific Crest Trail by Cheryl Strayed – In this memoir, a woman hikes over a thousand miles to try to process her mother's death, the breakdown of her marriage and the bad decisions she's made.

The Joys of Motherhood by Buchi Emecheta – A Nigerian woman raises her children in a time when colonial influences are beginning to challenge traditional tribal gender roles.

Stuck in the Middle with You: A Memoir of Parenting in Three Genders by Jennifer Finney Boylan – The memoir of a transgender woman transitioning from a father to a mother – and the period in between.

The Mothers by Sarah J Naughton – Five women, five secrets and one missing husband. A gripping psychological thriller.

Life After Life by Kate Atkinson – What if you had the chance to live your life again and again, until you finally got it right? One woman finds out as she lives (and re-lives) the turbulent events of the last century.

Motherhood by Sheila Heti – A candid novel about grappling with what it means to be a mother.

In what was formerly Yugoslavia, it was traditional for children to tie up their mum on Mother's Day. The only way she could get free was to 'pay' her children with treats. (This book is certainly not condoning such behaviour!)

Elizabeth Ann Buttle gave birth to her first child (a daughter) in May 1956. In November 1997, when Elizabeth was 60 years old, she gave birth to a son, making the babies 41 years apart. Quite an age gap!

The average amount spent on Mother's Day gifts varies depending on the country. In 2019, it was estimated that people spent approximately $186 in the US, $84 in Canada, €53 in France and £30 in the UK.

Newborns know their mother's voice at birth. When a baby is born, their hearing is impaired as the middle ear is still full of fluid. The only sound that they can recognize is their mother's voice.

In a large number of the world's languages, the word for 'mother' begins with the letter M. This is thought to be the result of it being one of the first sounds babies make.

Mother pandas keep contact with their cub nearly 100% of the time during the first month of the cub's life. The cub rests on her front and she covers it with her paw, arm or head.

Songs about
MUM

The special relationship with our mums has been the inspiration for an endless list of songwriters across all genres. What better way to celebrate the incredible and timeless impact mums make than through music? Our top 10 (in no particular order) will have every mum reaching for a tissue...

'The Hand That Rocks the Cradle' – by Glen Campbell

'The Wish' – Bruce Springsteen

'Mama Said' – The Shirelles

'Oh Mother' – Christina Aguilera

'Mama's Song' – by Carrie Underwood

'The Best Day' – Taylor Swift

'Mama' – Spice Girls

'Let It Be' – The Beatles

'Coat of Many Colors' – Dolly Parton

'Where You Lead' – Carole King

And two bonus tracks:

'Mother' – Kacey Musgraves

'Loves Me Like a Rock' – Paul Simon

It's a MYTH!

Mum myths get passed down through the generations. What your mum told you, you will one day repeat to your own children (if you haven't already). Strange thing is, most of us still believe these tall tales.

....

Myth: If you sit too close to the television it will ruin your eyes.

Truth: Sitting too close to the TV will not damage your eyes, but it may cause eye strain. Children can focus at close distance without eye strain better than adults. They often develop the habit of sitting right in front of the TV, although this stops as they get older.

Myth: If you eat sugar before bed, you'll never get to sleep.

Truth: Scientists say there is no evidence to prove that sugar causes instant hyperactivity. However, over time, eating large amounts of sugar can cause attention issues.

Myth: Don't swallow gum! It takes your body SEVEN years to digest it.

Truth: Gum is actually indigestible, so it just passes right through you at the same speed as everything else.

Myth: Eat up your carrots – they'll help you see in the dark.

Truth: Carrots contain vitamin A, which can improve your night vision, but only to the level of an ordinary healthy person. In World War II, to prevent Germany finding out that Britain was using radar to intercept bombers on night raids, the British issued press releases saying that pilots were eating lots of carrots to give them exceptional night vision. This fooled the British public, as well as German High Command, and so this myth was born!

Myth: When your fingers go wrinkly, it means it's time to get out of the water.

Truth: Your fingers start to wrinkle because they are adapting to their environment and improving your ability to grip things while wet – not because you've spent too long in the water.

Myth: Cracking your knuckles will give you arthritis.

Truth: The 'crack' of a knuckle is created by bubbles bursting in the fluid around your joints. There's no evidence that it's harmful, but it can be incredibly annoying for everyone else.

Myth: You need to wait 30–60 minutes after lunch before you go swimming.

Truth: This old wives' tale is based on the idea that the stomach will take away the oxygen needed by our muscles during swimming and cause cramping. In reality, people have more than enough oxygen to supply both the stomach and their muscles.

Myth: If you pick your nose and eat it, you'll get a huge bogey ball in your tummy and need to go to hospital.

Truth: Very unlikely. Some researchers say that eating bogies is actually good for you and can boost your immune system. Regardless of the health benefits, it's still best done in private!

Myth: If you pick a dandelion, you'll wet the bed.

Truth: Of course you won't! This myth stems from the fact that dandelions are a diuretic and diuretics increase the amount of urine that is released by the body. However, you'd have to eat the dandelion, not just touch it. And you'd probably have to eat quite a large quantity!

Our hero: real-life
SUPERMUMS

Never underestimate your strength

In 2009, Donna McNamee and Abigail Sicolo lifted a car off a young boy after he was run over in front of their home in England. The two women heard screams and ran out, thinking it may be one of their own children. When they saw the boy's legs under the car, without hesitating, they bent down to lift the car. The boy sustained injuries, but the two women saved his life.

A guardian angel

Lou Xiaoying was a hero in her native China. In 1972, she began rescuing newborn babies abandoned owing to China's one-child policy. The babies were all left to die in a rubbish dump near her home. Lou saved all the babies she found, nursed them back to health and raised them herself or adopted them out to friends and other family. She rescued her 30th baby when she was 82 years old.

Mum versus cougar

In 2017, a Canadian mum rescued her seven-year-old-son from a cougar in their backyard. She found her son on the ground, with the cougar firmly attached to his arm and dragging him away. The animal had jumped over a wire fence and pounced on the boy. Instinct took over and the brave mum leaped on the cougar, desperately trying to pry open its jaws with her hands and using every ounce of her physical strength. Eventually, the cougar let go and ran off. Thankfully, her son made a full recovery.

All about YOU

"A man loves his sweetheart the most,
his wife the best, but his mother the longest."

IRISH PROVERB

"[Motherhood is] the biggest gamble in the world.
It is the glorious life force. It's huge and scary
– it's an act of infinite optimism."

GILDA RADNER

"I believe the choice to become a mother is the choice to
become one of the greatest spiritual teachers there is."

OPRAH WINFREY

Bluff it:
CRAFTING

Ever been tempted to join a knitting circle? Or how about make your own clothes? Answer 'yes' to either of these questions and you've been nobbled by mum guilt. This is the feeling that you should know how to rustle up a dress using only straws and string. Here's your guide to faking it...

Firstly, Googling 'how to cheat at crafting' is a pointless exercise. You'll only end up with page upon page of Minecraft-related results. (No, we don't know either – you'll have to ask your kids.)

Homemade treats make great gifts. But do you really have the time or the inclination? Buy some biscuits from the shop and decant them from their packaging. Next, place them in a clear food bag. Cut a strip of wrapping paper to the same width as the bag, fold it over the top and staple. Find yourself a fancy gift tag and fix it to the bag. Ta da!

If you're attempting to make clothes for yourself, get someone else to take your measurements – it's downright impossible to do it yourself properly. And get them to take the measurements twice (or even three times), just to be on the safe side.

Okay, so you're desperate to have a go at making yourself a patterned dress. Stop! Do you know how complicated it is to match patterns up across seams?!? It's way above your pay grade, so keep it as simple as possible for yourself and start off with a PLAIN fabric.

Go with what you know. If you can remember from school how to make pompoms using a ring of card and a ball of wool, go for it! You can create a whole range of fancy things with pompoms.

Puckering. Nope, not the permanent look that Alpha mums get after too many lip fillers. This is much more serious. Puckering is what happens to fabric when you pull stitches too tight. It'll give you away as an amateur – so know your own strength.

Can't be bothered with sewing on a badge? Fabric glue is the sanity-saving alternative. DO NOT BE TEMPTED TO USE SUPERGLUE to make sure it really, really sticks. Guaranteed, the glue will go somewhere you didn't intend it to. Did you know that just a small amount of superglue is strong enough to lift a two-ton jeep off the ground?

If you find yourself really struggling, there are kits available to get you started. Try friendship bracelets, candle making or flower pressing as an easy introduction to crafting. NOTE: we're talking here about the kits for kids. Easy-to-read instructions and simple to follow – no one need ever know. Just make sure you have an adult around to help you with using the scissors!

Treat yourself:
FACE YOGA

You'll need to accept that this will make
you look ridiculous. Mind you, looking like
you're trying to get spinach out of your
teeth is far outweighed by the benefits of
face yoga. The idea is to activate and build
the muscles in your face so that it's less
likely to sag – making your face appear
fuller and more youthful. Give it a try...

Exercise #1: Deep stretch and de-wrinkler

Keeping your shoulders back and relaxed, point your chin down to your chest and make an oval with your mouth. Look upward with just your eyes and hold for three seconds. Tuck your upper lip inside your mouth and make an 'ahhh' face.

Exercise #2: Cheek lift

No, not *those* cheeks! Leave those for Kim K. Open the mouth to form an 'O', pull your upper lip up over your top teeth and then smile to lift your cheek muscles up. Place your fingers on the top part of your cheek, release the muscles to lower them and then lift them back up. Repeat several times.

Exercise #3: Eyebrow lift

Smile and then press three fingertips of each hand under your eyebrows to force your eyes open. Try to frown your eyebrows down against your fingers, then close your eyelids tightly and roll your eyeballs upward. (Go steady if you're wearing contact lenses!) Hold for 20 seconds.

Exercise #4: Forehead lift

Interlace your hands. Placing your fingers over your forehead, apply light pressure and attempt to lift your forehead. Repeat 50 times. You can also try holding it for one minute. Alternatively, place both palms on your temples, push your palms up and back to lift the sides of your face. Hold for five seconds and keep repeating.

Exercise #5: Eye opener

Use your fingers to form a 'glasses' shape around your eyes, encompassing your eyebrows and cheeks. Lift your eyebrows (trying not to wrinkle your forehead too much), squint and then lift them again. Repeat 50 times.

Exercise #6: Double-chin buster

Place your elbows on a table or on your knees. Place your fists (or your thumbs) under your chin and press them upwards whilst opening your mouth. Hold for five seconds and then repeat 5–10 times.

Exercise #7: Lion's breath

This well-known yoga breathing exercise helps to relax the face muscles and reduce stress. Sit in a comfortable position and place your hands on your knees. Inhale deeply. When you exhale, open your mouth wide, poke your tongue out towards your chin and make a 'ha' sound. The 'ha' should come from your throat. Complete the breathing cycle for one minute and then relax. Repeat three times.

Exercise #8: Cheek toner

Tilt your head back until you're staring at the ceiling. Suck your cheeks in as far you can, just as if you're making a fish face. Hold this pose for five seconds – your cheeks will start to ache! Repeat 10–15 times.

Don't ask your KIDS

We love to bombard our kids with questions: How was your day? Have you done your homework? What time do you call this?! But are there questions that a mum just shouldn't ask? Ignorance can be bliss if the answer is not what you expected (and you'd rather not have known).

"Does this outfit look okay?"

"Who do you love more? Me or YouTube?"

"What do you like best about your friends' mums?"

"What do I do that embarrasses you most?"

"What's the worst thing you've ever done and not told me about?"

"Can you see any grey hairs?"

"If we were the same age, would you be my friend?"

"Do you worry that you'll turn into me?"

"If you could change one thing about me, what would it be?"

"If you were me, how would you do it?"

"How about we make a TikTok video together?"

"Would you like to clean your room or shall I do it?"

"What is it like being my son/daughter?"

"Is that enough money or do you need more?"

"If you could choose a nickname for me, what would it be?"

For the mum who has EVERYTHING

Gifts for mums are carefully thought-out... sometimes. The reality is that, whilst well-meaning, they can be a little repetitive, usually making Mum or her home smell lovely. All well and good, but what about alternative ideas to spice up Mother's Day, birthdays and Christmas? Think outside the box... (Mums – leave this page open where the family can see it.)

MUMTASTIC – WHY YOU'RE SO AWESOME

Goodbye flowers that die after a week... hello beautiful
spring bulbs that will pop up year after year.

Say "no" to bubble bath... and "yes" to a spa day.

Forget a giant cookie iced with her name... and fill a hamper
with all her favourite food, treats and drinks.

Not another candle... how about restaurant vouchers
for a candlelit dinner for two?

How lovely, a scarf... but a trip to Mum's favourite shop
to choose her own is even lovelier.

One more boxset for the pile...
why not take her out to the cinema?

More chocolates?... a chocolate-making workshop
would be much sweeter.

Another leather-bound keepsake book... go shoe shopping
for leather that won't get so dusty.

'World's Best Mum' mug... only really says 'World's Tackiest Gift',
so save your money for an afternoon tea instead.

Why do mother kangaroos hate rainy days?
Because their kids have to play inside.

My 'mum voice' was so loud even my neighbours brushed
their teeth, put their shoes on and got in my car.

When your children are teenagers, get a dog – it's important
to have someone in the house who's happy to see you.

Whenever you find yourself feeling like a bad mother, just
remember that the mum in *Home Alone* was halfway to Paris
before she realized that they were missing a child.

10 ways to give yourself
A BREAK

If you're forever beating yourself up for not being a good enough parent, join the Mum Club! Mums can be their own worst enemy. You know that you don't function well when you're stressed, so it's time to give yourself a break. Try these 10 ways to switch off and recharge your batteries.

1. Meditate away the chatter in your head. Practising meditation teaches you to quieten the stream of thoughts that run through your head like a steam train. Meditation encourages clarity of mind, allowing you to better manage your thoughts and worries.

2. Keep a gratitude journal. This can help you see the joys in life and put things in perspective. Set aside time each day to write down what made you happy and feel good that day. Even if you only spend five minutes on it, you'll soon see an increase in your positive thinking and more resilience to the challenges mumhood throws at you.

3. Unwind by 'forest bathing'. This is the Japanese practice of immersing yourself in nature and fully engaging with your senses to experience everything around you – the birds singing, the warmth of the sun on your face or the breeze on your skin. Take a slow meander through a forest or woodland and soak up the calming atmosphere.

4. Make a conscious effort to set aside time for a hobby. It could be learning a language, restoring furniture, reading or drawing. It doesn't matter how badly you do it, what matters is focusing on something that's just for YOU. Anything that breaks your usual routine and gives you a sense of achievement will do wonders for your soul.

5. *Shavasana* – also known in yoga as the 'corpse pose' – relaxes and rejuvenates every muscle in the body and calms the nervous system. Lie on your back with your arms by your sides and your legs outstretched. Do nothing, stay still and breathe deeply. If thoughts come into your head, just watch them pass. After 15 minutes, come to life again slowly, wriggling your fingers and toes, and have a big stretch.

6. Whether you dust off your bike and freewheel down a hill, or simply go for a brisk walk around the block, cardio exercise helps reduce stress and encourages a better night's sleep. Just getting out into the open air can be enough to clear your head and blow away your worries.

7. Take half an hour out to give someone a call. Yes, a call, not a text! It could be a friend you've not spoken to in ages or a person you know will make you giggle. Your feel-good serotonin levels will start flowing, giving you a short-term hug! In the long term, keeping in touch with people ensures you have a strong support network.

8. If you've got a willing volunteer, have a cuddle and a kiss! It will increase the level of the love chemical oxytocin in your blood. Oxytocin is the chemical released during childbirth to help mums bond with their baby – thankfully, cuddles are pain-free and don't leave you sitting on a 'special cushion' for days afterwards.

9. Do a body scan. Sit or lie somewhere comfortable and quiet. Slow your breath. Starting at the top of your head, focus on relaxing each part of your body, working your way down to the tip of your toes. We carry stress in parts of our body without realizing it – the body scan encourages deep relaxation. The process should last around 20 minutes.

10. Give yourself a day off for good behaviour! Even if it's just a few hours when the kids are at school or between coming home from work and bedtime, forget chores, switch off your phone and just do things for YOU. Or do nothing! Mums can be too hard on themselves, failing to make enough time to relax and take stock of their achievements. Gifting yourself some time off is a great way to acknowledge that you deserve it.

All about
YOU

"There's no way to be a perfect mother
and a million ways to be a good one."

JILL CHURCHILL

"Grown don't mean nothing to a mother.
A child is a child. They get bigger, older,
but grown. In my heart it don't mean a thing."

TONI MORRISON

"Motherhood is the exquisite inconvenience
of being another person's everything."

UNKNOWN

Regardless of whether they are left- or right-handed, human mothers tend to cradle their babies on the left side of their bodies. The brain's right hemisphere is where emotions are processed, so holding a baby on the left may help transmit social information to the right side more efficiently.

Blue whale mothers need to produce 50 gallons of milk per day in order to feed their babies. After calves are born, they grow rapidly and gain 200 pounds in weight per day!

In 2020, in the US alone, $26.7 billion was spent on Mother's Day. This compares to the $17 billion that was spent on Father's Day.

A study of the pregnancies of more than 30,000 German women found that pregnancy spreads in workplaces. In the year after a colleague had a baby, there was an increase in first pregnancies in the same office. The 'pregnancy chair' in your office might not be such a joke after all!

In China, it is traditional for new mums to stay in the house for the first month after their baby is born. This is so they can be spoilt by relatives. (And probably go stir crazy!)

In the first year of a child's life, a mum changes around 7,300 nappies and washes around 5,000 items of baby clothing.

The earliest record of celebrating mums can be traced back to 250 BC when the ancient Romans held a festival known as 'Hilaria'. The three-day festival honoured the mother goddess, Cybele, with parties, games and offerings at the temple.

Bluff it:
POPULAR CULTURE

Does talking to your kids leave you confused at times? You think you understand what they're talking about, but not quite enough to maintain a conversation. And if you do try, you end up showing yourself up and getting ridiculed. Never fear, we're going to tell you a few things you need to know about popular culture to pass yourself off as a 'quite cool mum'...

Music. Once upon a time, there were lots of songs sung by different singers/bands. These days there are still lots of songs, but they all sound like they're sung by the same person. Some of your old favourites are creeping out of the woodwork to supplement their pensions – sadly, the material they're producing makes your kids wonder how on earth they ever made it big. To sound like you've got the finger on the pulse, remember names like Dua Lipa, Doja Cat and Lil Nas X. In fact, if you get stuck, just string together some letters together, e.g. Dyra Fats, Jus K Derb or Dipy Loli.

Sport. Remember when the Olympics was all about the athletics? Nowadays, they're chock-a-block with every event imaginable. The 2020 Olympics saw the introduction of sport climbing. This includes climbing up a wall as fast as you can. A bit like the mums' race at school sports day, but on a vertical surface and with fewer broken legs. Fact to impress the kids: breakdancing has been confirmed as an Olympic sport for Paris 2024.

Television/film. You might still sit down at a particular time to watch a TV show 'live', but your kids 'stream' their entertainment now. Don't show your age by saying, "Have you watched the latest series?". A 'series' is now popularly known as a 'season'. (Thankfully, the programmes that make up a 'season' are still called 'episodes'.) Many of the films you enjoyed in your youth have now been remade and feature trendier folk with sophisticated gadgets. Cool show to know: *Squid Game*. (It has nothing to do with seafood.)

TikTok is a video-sharing app that features an endless barrage of videos made by TikTok users. Videos can be a maximum of 15 seconds or they can be combined to make them into 60 seconds (of joy or drivel – it spans both). As a parent, you're very cool if you know about TikTok. However, it would be incredibly uncool to set up an account and attempt to post your own videos.

Facebook. If you want to be down with the kids, don't let on that you still use Facebook. According to the TikTok generation, Facebook is for the oldies. If you find yourself about to declare you read something on Facebook (gasp!), stop yourself. Replace 'on Facebook' with 'somewhere' and save yourself any embarrassment. The great thing about your kids not using Facebook is that you can post whatever you like about them on there and they'll never know.

Chat-up lines for SINGLE MUMS

Dating isn't easy for anyone. It's even harder if you're a single mum. The good news is that having kids can be a great way to meet a future soulmate – just make them part of the conversation. Copy the chat-up lines below and pop them in your pocket. You never know when they might be useful...

"Have you got a wipe/nappy/plaster I could have, please?"

"Do you come to this playground often?"

"If you weren't a parent, what type of car would you drive?"

"Your son/daughter is gorgeous – they must take after you."

"Have we met before? I think our children were at school together."

"I can't remember the last time I went out for dinner with adults…"

"Should I tell my kids' babysitter that I'm going to be home late?"

"How about a play date?"

"Could I sit with you at the PTA meeting tonight?
I find some of the school mums a bit scary."

"I make a mean bolognese with no bits in it.
I can make an extremely mild curry too."

"My kids told me I need to get out and meet someone
who'll make me smile again. I think it's you."

"Do you have any raisins? Or how about a date?"

"My kids showed me all the filters on Snapchat –
but you're living proof that filters aren't needed."

"My son said he'd found a funny, clever partner for me. Is it you?"

What type of mum ARE YOU?

Every mum is special in their own unique way. That said, we probably all recognize certain 'tribes' of mums, either from amongst our friends or from the endless events we've had no choice but to attend as the kids have grown up. What type of mum do you think you are? Be honest! Ask your kids too, if you dare – they might have a very different perspective!

Earth mother

You wake naturally – no alarm clock for you – and slip into something floaty that you bought at a festival in the summer. After brushing the long locks of your six children, you all sit on the floor to enjoy the organic granola you've soaked overnight before setting off on the three-mile bike ride to school. You might secretly flinch at the sugary, processed food other parents feed their kids, but you're too polite to say anything.

Most likely to say: "It's only natural that they're a bit naughty when the moon is in its waxing phase."

Perfectionist mum

Anxious about appearance, you're the mum most likely to be found in full make-up on ANY occasion. Your children excel in all the activities you've signed them up to – and will go on to have 'very good jobs'. Fully committed to everything you do, you're the first choice for running the PTA. You can be hypercritical and set yourself unrealistically high parenting standards.

Most likely to say: "What do you mean, 'It's okay to be "good enough"'?

Free-range mum

You don't micromanage your kids' lives and are comfortable for them to find their own way (both physically and spiritually) and learn from their own mistakes. Often to be found trying to locate a child that was 'there a minute ago', you turn up to playdates with a bottle of wine and leave when you realize your kids have already gone home by themselves. 'Laid back' is your middle name.

Most likely to say: "I definitely came out with three children..."

Competitive mum

When you're not running your own highly successful business, you're sitting in on your children's cello and piano recitals. The biggest cake at the bake sale, the most elaborate papier-mâché school project – these are all down to you. You were the most vocal supporter at all your children's sports fixtures until you were banned for not being able to accept defeat gracefully. If anyone's kids achieve something brilliant, you always have a story to tell of how yours did it better.

Most likely to say: "My child walked at three months and had a full set of teeth at five months."

Party mum

When your children arrived, life didn't change for you. As soon as you've put the kids to bed, your fellow party mums are at the door clutching bottles of prosecco and feather boas. Any social event organized on a weeknight that ends up messily can be traced back to you. You have a reliable babysitter on speed dial who knows you won't find your keys when you get home and who opens the door before you start calling through the letter box and wake the kids up.

Most likely to say: "Shall I bring the wine?"

Frazzled mum

You're tired. So very, very tired ALL the time. You stumble through motherhood half-asleep, somehow managing to get everything done, yet not remembering that you've done it. Sometimes, you stare at other mothers through lidded eyes and wonder how they found time to change out of their pyjamas, let alone put make-up on. Whilst you love your family, there's nothing you wouldn't give for a weekend away by yourself.

Most likely to say: "I can't remember the last time I had eight hours' sleep."

Sporty mum

Always in sportswear (and not just because it's comfy). When other mums bump into you, you're either on your way to a gym class or have completed a 10k run before breakfast. Your energy levels mean you parent like a whirlwind, bounding from one challenge to the next – and nailing it. You measure your success through how many mums you've recruited to join you on your 6am run. This might be why sometimes it feels like people avoid you...

Most likely to say: "I've done three spin classes and 30,000 steps today."

Perfect mum

You like to get everything spot on and tick all the 'things I must do as a mother' boxes – whether it's the cutest wellies for your toddlers or a family photoshoot with your grown-up kids, complete with white linen shirts. Your children are exquisitely behaved, polite and opt for nutritious snacks to see them through their long list of extra-curricular activities. You are very, very nice but do be aware that you might make other mums feel inadequate.

Most likely to say: "I've just ordered our matching family Christmas pyjamas – and it's only July!"

A mum's guide to
TEXTING

Who said text acronyms are
just for teenagers? If you're trying to
simultaneously finish a work presentation,
cook dinner and send a text, don't
waste time on unnecessary wordage
when an acronym will do.

....

SILB: Still in laundry basket

HIB: Hiding in bathroom

YNGOLT: You're not going out like that

WAY: Where are you?

AYEL: Are you even listening?

IANYS: I am not your slave

WTON: Wet towel on floor

AYF: Ask your father

TDNW: The dog needs walking

RFOPOD: Raid fridge on pain of death

ILYB: I love you, but ...

KDMC: Kids driving me crazy

BC: Before children

SIOB: Sharp intake of breath

IIBY: Is it bedtime yet?

HLLAH: House looks like a hellhole

RLA: Running late again

The last WORD

"It's the three pairs of eyes that mothers have to have. One pair that sees through closed doors. Another in the back of her head and, of course, the ones in front that can look at a child when he goofs up and reflect 'I understand and I love you' without so much as uttering a word."

Erma Bombeck